What Every Boss Needs to Know
Learning to Keep Your Frog in Your Pocket

Dedication

This is dedicated to Sigrid and Sydney, who put up with us as we worked through the process of developing and completing this book.

WHAT EVERY BOSS NEEDS TO KNOW

Learning to Keep Your Frog in Your Pocket

Wallace R. Johnston & Linda C. Martin

Revised edition, copyright ©2006
First edition ©2001
JOB TALK LLC
P.O. Box 4599
Richmond, VA 23220
All rights reserved.

No part of this publication may be reproduced or transmitted in any form or by any means, electronic or mechanical, including photocopying, recording or by any information storage and retrieval system, without permission in writing from JOB TALK LLC.

What Every Boss Needs to Know:
Learning to Keep Your Frog in Your Pocket
by Wallace R. Johnston and Linda C. Martin.
Artwork by Robert Edwards.

Published and printed in the United States of America.

ISBN 978-1-84728-757-1

Table of Contents

Acknowledgements v
About the Authors vii
    Linda Martin
    Wallace Johnston
Introduction ix
    Speaking of Work
The Frog 1
When You're a Frog... 3
The Performance Formula 7
    The Variables 8
        Employee Attributes.. 9
        Energy 10
        The Boss 11
    Putting the Variables Together 12
    The Challenge 13
Part One: EMPLOYEE ATTRIBUTES.. 15
    Attitudes.. 16
    Creativity 18
    Education vs. Maturity 21
    Personal Interests... 23
    Locus of Control 26
    Part One Summary... 29

Part Two: ENERGY 33
    Structure 34
    Motivation 37
    Part Two Summary 40

Part Three: THE BOSS 43
    Experience 44
    Teams 47
    Diversity 49
    Self-Fulfilling Prophecy 52
    Communication 54
    Trust 57
    Part Three Summary 60

Performance Formula Recap 63
30 Frog-like Behaviors 65

Note: Throughout this text, personal pronouns and character examples are alternately presented as male and female, randomly. No inference is intended to be made about gender, and in all cases, behaviors can be considered equally applicable to men and women.

Acknowledgements

We want to thank all of the "frogs" who have made our efforts possible. Our gratitude goes to all of those people who can recognize the frog in others, but not in themselves. We empathize with you—you are not alone. It happens to the best of us.

A special thanks to those who read and reviewed and assisted in the development and process of this book. We value all of the input and feedback we received along the way.

About the Authors

Linda Martin

Linda Martin has over twenty years of leadership experience in education, training and development in the public sector, computer industry and health care. She is certified as a Senior Professional in Human Resources. She first met Dr. Johnston while working on her Masters in Business Administration at Virginia Commonwealth University. After many years, she reconnected with Dr. Johnston as a co-author. In addition to her work with Dr. Wally, Ms. Martin is the Director of Human Resources Development for a health care system and is writing a book designed to assist leaders in assessing their effectiveness through reflective writing. She resides in Richmond, Virginia with her daughter, Sydney, their two cats, and Sara, the dog.

Wallace Johnston

Dr. Wallace Johnston is a syndicated columnist, commentator and speaker. His weekly columns are *Speaking of Work* and *Ask Dr. Wally*. As a commentator and speaker, his focus is on contemporary work and work place issues. He has written extensively on management and employee development, communication skills and teamwork. He released a CD, *Messages for Self*, in 2000, and his first book, *Speaking of Work*, two years earlier. Dr. Johnston earned his degree from the George Washington University and holds Emeritus status from the School of Business at Virginia Commonwealth University. He and his wife, Sigrid, reside in Richmond, Virginia and Telluride, Colorado. "Dr. Wally" can always be found at www.askdrwally.com.

Introduction

Speaking of Work

This is a simple book with some not-so-simple thoughts. It does not offer an in-depth study of the topics, since there are hundreds of books out there on any one of them. Our intention is to provide a place for a boss (or anyone who wants to be a boss) to start thinking about what it means to be a boss, or perhaps a way to review some basic management issues.

We've chosen the word "boss" over "manager" because we believe management tends to focus on things. And this book is definitely not about things. When we use boss, all of us know that we are referring to that person who affects our work in big ways. If you are a boss, or desire to be one, we hope that as you explore this little book, you begin to create a clearer picture of yourself, that you have a laugh or two, and ultimately perhaps even boss more effectively.

We wrote this book to address issues that bosses face on a daily basis. Using the Performance Formula, we isolate variables that directly impact work. Bosses deal with these variables or work issues over and over. They have direct control over some, but for the most part they only have an indirect influence. However, this indirect influence is critical as they rely on their employees to do the job and do it well. By using the Performance Formula, we show the relationships between work, the boss and the employee, and the potential outcomes.

Although all the variables relate to one another, we discuss them as independents. By doing so, we think you will be able to see more clearly the impact of desired and undesired behaviors in the workplace on all the variables.

We believe that bosses develop mindsets that both help and hinder work. Our quest is to present material that can help improve the boss. Traps, misunderstandings, perceptual sets and experience are fields for examination and reexamination.

As you read through the book, we know you will find kernels to reinforce current positive boss behaviors and some that will cause you to rethink your behaviors.

We start out with the metaphor of the frog to show a boss's (or an employee's) capacity to react to situations. We will revisit the metaphor of the frog throughout the book to point out dysfunctional behaviors.

The Frog

Most bosses are familiar with the parable of the boiling frog. If you put a frog in boiling water, it will immediately jump out. Put it in water at room temperature, gradually heat the water, and the unsuspecting frog will cook. From this story, we learn an important lesson: Always be alert and attuned to your environment; don't be lulled into a false sense of safety. Frogs and bosses have a lot in common. Think about the bosses you know who have become complacent in their work only to have it come back to haunt them. Like frogs, few survive without adapting to the changes in their environment.

Wait! There is more to learn from the frog.

As you probably already know, frogs, for the most part, are non-adaptive. Take them away from their habitat and their survival rate is low. Their eating habits are "random." They're not sure where to look for food, so they hop around randomly. They don't have a clear goal. They just hop around until they find something, or they sit and wait for food to come to them. Eating is usually a matter of being in the right place at the right time. Now you may know a few bosses who have succeeded without goals and by just waiting for opportunities to come to them, but chances are that most have not made it.

Frogs are also reactive. To get a frog to jump, you only have to make a loud noise, or poke it and it will react by moving forward. That's the only way frogs can move—forward, in the direction they're facing. Now, that can be a problem. If the frog is facing a fan and you make a loud noise, well, you know about things that hit the fan. Like frogs, some bosses can only move in one direction and their reactions are predictable. It doesn't take long for an employee to figure this out. You can imagine what happens to a boss when an employee, or for that matter a co-worker, knows how to make him jump.

When You're a Frog

Being a frog limits your chances of success, especially in today's environment of increased competition and constant change. You spend your time reacting rather than acting. The result may be declining production, declining revenues and increased pressures. Soon you, your department or the whole organization begins to resemble frogs, randomly hopping around, gigging others and getting gigged in return—yes, a veritable frog farm.

Too often bosses blame their failures on employees: not enough employees, unmotivated employees, employees with bad attitudes, and so on. But where does it really start? It starts with the boss and his or her failure to do the following four things:

1. Failure to recognize and accept variability in human behavior. Why do we want everyone to act like us? By increasing your comfort level with the uncertainties of human behavior and better accommodating an extensive range of behavior, you can become more successful. Too often bosses have either unrealistic expectations or vague expectations. They define successful performance for themselves, and for others, as perfection. Perfection is a unique situation and is seldom maintained. Even excellent baseball players who make millions of dollars only hit the ball one third of the time, at best. Solution: Understand and accept yourself and others.

2. Failure to adapt to the environment. Environment is composed of a number of attributes: structure, goals, and management issues such as employee relations and benefits. Do you change structure so your employees can be more successful? Do you continue to move in the same direction even when you know things aren't working? In other words, are you a frog heading for the fan? It's up to you to determine the structure that's needed to get the job done. Solution: Clarify goals and expectations.

3. Failure to recognize the ambiguity of words. Words are loaded. Take the word "morale." How often do you talk with other bosses about morale? What is morale? And does good morale necessarily equate to good performance? We know bad morale and poor performance go hand-in-hand. There have been multiple studies that confirm this relationship. But do we know the reverse is true? How about when you assign an employee a task and say, "I need this ASAP," are your meaning and the employee's meaning the same? When they do what they think you wanted, but it isn't, do you gig them? Solution: Define words. Say what you mean and assure understanding.

4. Failure to know what makes your frog jump. It's funny when you realize that almost anyone else can figure it out. What really gets you going, gets a reaction out of you? The employee who is continuously late to work? The unmotivated employee? The one who does the bare minimum to get by? The one who disagrees with you or is always complaining? Keeping your frog under control starts with you. Solution: Know yourself.

Quit acting like a frog! To stop acting like a frog is sometimes difficult. Did you recognize yourself in any of the behaviors in the last section? Understanding a few basic concepts underlying employee and boss behavior increases your chances for improvement. Your success as a boss depends on your ability to overcome your limiting behaviors, to stop being surprised by other people's behaviors and to stop acting like a frog. Learn to recognize when your frog is ready to start hopping and find a way to keep it in your pocket. Before you go any further, you might want to get yourself a small toy frog from the nature store, or cut out a little frog from the back page of this book. Keep it in your pocket—just as a reminder.

We all have things that trigger our reactive behaviors and emotions, things that will set us off. What are your triggers? What are the things that will set your frog in motion? How do you know when the frog has taken over? How quickly can you get the frog back in your pocket? What actions do you need to take?

Keep your frog in your pocket!

If you find this a challenge, you may want to explore the topic of cognitive distortions and how to disrupt negative thinking.

Let's start with the Performance Formula.

This simple three-variable formula sums up what all bosses need to remember if they want to reach performance goals and keep from acting like frogs.

The Performance Formula

Performance =
Employee Attributes x
Energy x
the Boss

Performance in an organization results from a symbiotic relationship.

It isn't you, and it isn't me. It's us.

The Variables

In the Performance Formula, if any variable is low, the overall performance is low. All of the variables are interdependent. As you study each variable, think carefully about your staff and yourself. What are the strengths and weaknesses? What do you need to do differently?

Employee Attributes

Employee attributes are those qualities an employee brings to the work place, such as experience, knowledge, education, ability to get along, desire to perform, IQ, thinking and reasoning abilities, attitudes, creativity, maturity, personality, and locus of control. These represent the employee dimensions that make up the Performance Formula. How can you affect these?

Your best shot is in hiring the right people from the start. It's not too difficult to identify experience and skills, but what about other qualities like creativity and desire to perform? These represent performance skills and ultimately are more critical to an employee's success than their technical skills. What do you need in an employee? How clear is your profile? Hiring is not a subject to be taken lightly.

Your next best chance after hiring the right people is giving them the training they need to develop their skills. Every organization is different, so it's your responsibility to help new employees know what you want and how you want it. It doesn't matter if they have zero experience or ten years of experience. Training can take place in the classroom, through your one-on-one guidance, or using the buddy system—whatever works. One thing is for sure: training can't be left to chance. The method and content need to be planned and then delivered.

Energy

Energy comes from an employee's motivation, as well as the processes for getting the work done. Is the employee a high energy person, or do they do the minimum necessary to get by? What's your own level of commitment and enthusiasm? Are your systems and processes designed in such a way that you get the greatest possible output from the expenditure of energy?

That last one is an important question. When was the last time your employees asked, "Why are we doing this?" or "Is there a better way?" You better hope they are asking these questions, because if they aren't, you're going to be left behind. Better yet, if they aren't asking, why aren't they? Are you inhibiting their contributions?

The Boss

How you perform as the boss is strictly within your domain. How do you treat your employees? Do they feel respected? Can you be trusted? Is communication clear and adequate? Are you consistent? Do you walk the talk?

It's up to you as the boss to:

- Select the right people and train them.
- Expect differences.
- Create appropriate structures.
- Define clear goals and expectations.
- Monitor performance.
- Treat people with respect.
- Communicate.
- Know yourself, and...
- Keep your frog under control.

Putting the Variables Together

Let's look at how the three variables—employee attributes, energy, and the boss—work together. The following is a true story. The names have been changed to protect the innocent, Shelby, the employee, and the not-so-innocent boss, George.

Shelby & George

Shelby (the employee) was a bright person who had the experience and the skills (employee attributes) to do a good job. But her work was consistently below quality. She was slow starting on projects and seemed to flounder (energy). George (the boss) was frustrated. He met with Shelby over and over to discuss these problems. He supported her, he encouraged her, he tried simple projects, and he tried disciplinary actions. He thought he was fair and a good boss. He was, but he was still acting like a frog. He was reacting to the situation, and he was reacting to Shelby.

Keep your frog in your pocket!

Then one day George thought, "Maybe the problem isn't with Shelby. Maybe it's with me." He figured out that Shelby needed more structure and clearer communication. Before long George was able to turn the situation around, and Shelby became one of his best performers.

Does this sound like a fairy tale? We promise it's not. It happened.

The Challenge

As you read through the following sections, see if you can identify performance factors that you have taken for granted or that may be missing. When you see the little frog, be on the lookout for potential frog behaviors.

Ask yourself

- Which ones send me jumping?
- What do I have to do differently?
- What do I have to reevaluate?
- What am I doing right?

While the answers will point you in a direction, you will have to engage in the process of changing your mindset and/or behavior for there to be a difference. In other words, you have to learn to keep your frog in your pocket and not let it take control.

In the Performance Formula, employee attributes are those qualities and characteristics each individual worker brings to the workplace.

In one way or another, each one will impact performance.

Part One

Performance =
Employee Attributes x
Energy x
the Boss

In Part One, we examine
Employee Attributes:

Attitudes
Creativity
Education vs. Maturity
Personal Interests
Locus of Control

Why can't every employee be like me?

Attitudes

Good ones are like mine.

Did you know that 77 percent of people in a survey acknowledged that they could work harder than they do? Now you're probably thinking, "Aha! I was right. I need to do something about these employees and their attitudes." That mindset is frog-like! Remember, the survey wasn't just about them. It's about you, too.

Unfortunately, there is a human tendency to think that an employee has a bad attitude when his attitude doesn't match up to ours. In reality, almost no one goes around saying, "I've got a really rotten attitude and I need to change it." Anyway, what do you mean when you say someone has an attitude? Attitudes are intangible.

Sally & Bill

Usually, when we're talking about an attitude, we are making inferences based on behaviors we've witnessed. For example, Sally comes to work on time every day with a terrific smile on her face. Her boss says she has a great attitude. Notice that this says nothing about Sally's productivity. Her productivity may not be that great, but it's likely that her boss won't notice, because her attitude appears so positive.

On the other hand, Bill comes in late many days and often grouses about, rarely smiling and barely greeting anyone. Bill is one of the most productive employees in the group, never misses a deadline, and you can count on the quality of his work. Your problem is that he's an irritant to everyone else. Other employees complain to you about his unfriendliness and how difficult it is to work with him. You think he has a bad attitude and want him to do something about it. You may think about his attitude so much that you forget about his work. If you confront Bill, it's likely he will tell you that he doesn't have a bad attitude, he gets his work done and does more than anyone else in the department. This is a dilemma! You may ask yourself, "Why can't I have both—a good attitude and productive work?"

Keep your frog in your pocket!

You can have both, but first you have to determine what qualifies as a good attitude in your department and how you will know it when you see it. Translate attitude into behaviors. It's very unlikely you can reach agreement with an employee about his or her attitude, but you can reach agreement about behaviors—the actions you expect to see. Is it really important that everyone smiles when they come in, or is it more important that they acknowledge each other and are courteous? You can even engage your employees in a discussion that lets them define how they want to be treated by each other. They can identify the "social" norms for the group.

If you want to see changes in attitudes, get people to change their behaviors. When behaviors change, attitudes will usually follow.

Creativity

We all have the capacity, but...

A number of years ago, a group of psychologists conducted a study examining the level of creativity in adults. According to the study, only about 5 percent of the adults age 40 and over demonstrated a high degree of creativity. As the age was lowered, there was no significant increase in creativity until the psychologists studied a group of 17-year-olds. Their creativity scores increased to an impressive 10 percent. However, when the psychologists worked with a group of 5-year-olds, over 90 percent demonstrated creativity. Now, there are all kinds of things that can be read into this study, but no matter how you cut it, it's obvious that most of us were creative in the beginning. So what happened?

The reality is, our society places a lot more value on having the "right" answer than on being creative. Our schools emphasize being "right" rather than asking questions or coming up with creative solutions to problems. We carry this behavior into the work force.

Creativity thrives when there are few limits, minimal structure, a willingness to be wrong, and acceptance of mistakes. Very few organizations are ready for this. Very few are willing to forego structure and allow the freedom that creativity requires.

If you go by an employee's desk and she is staring off into space for a half hour, you start worrying about productivity and think the employee is lazy. Creativity takes "think" time, time to stare into space and let the brain rumble around. We must ask ourselves, do we really want creativity among our employees, or do we just want them to look in the "right" ways to find the "right" answers to problems?

If you decide you want creativity, then you've got to be willing to "create" an environment conducive to it. You must accept that not every creative moment reaches fruition, and not every creative moment contributes directly to the bottom line. But when a magic moment takes place, watch out for what comes next.

Often bosses turn off to creative ideas because they believe an employee's ideas are impractical. What they don't realize is that in their process of turning off, they also turn off the employee's enthusiasm and motivation.

Mary & Sam

Consider Mary. Mary is an excellent employee. She works hard and is always coming up with new ideas. Recently, she complained to her boss, Sam, that her ideas weren't being used. She was upset—ready to gig a frog. Sam told her some of her ideas weren't very good and some had not been studied. His frog was jumping.

What could he do instead? If the boss wants to keep Mary creating, he could start asking Mary to think about how her ideas could be implemented. In other words, she needs to be guided to the next creative step—the practical implementation of an idea. New ideas are great, but they are of little value if they are not implemented. Getting the idea generator to follow through and examine the feasibility of an idea is a great learning tool. With Mary taking this step, she will increase her value as an employee. Rather than becoming frustrated, she will continue to be creative and add to the department's success.

Keep your frog in your pocket!

If people are not as creative as you like, or too creative for the circumstances, think through what is happening. What else do they need to know? How can you lead them to the next step? Don't be a frog and just react. Be creative yourself.

Education vs. Maturity

A twenty-year-old is still a twenty-year-old.

The work force is changing. It always has been! Bosses complain the only thing their younger employees want is to have a good time, that they don't seem to have any commitment. Often bosses seem to think if the employee graduated from college he should be very responsible. That may or may not be the case. Most "twenty-somethings" aren't too worried about tomorrow and certainly aren't thinking about retirement.

How quickly these bosses forget: they were once young, too. They brought to the work force a different outlook and a level of energy that gave their predecessors difficulty. Now, in the same position, today's bosses have short memories.

The up-and-coming work force has expectations. Most employees want to work and grow. But, like past generations they have their own terms. After all, they are smarter and more informed than previous generations at similar ages and stages of life.

BUT, they are not more mature. Most twenty-year-olds today have less responsibility than a twenty-year-old a decade ago. Numerous books have been written about the modern trend toward delaying adulthood. Young and inexperienced workers relate to work from a low maturity level. They may have education or intelligence, but they do not have the experience or perspective that the boss has.

Experience helps employees mature. They learn that what's in the book may or may not always work. Experience and time help them to gain greater patience with others, which makes them better employees.

The boss's goal, then, is to create an environment in which the younger employee can mature and gain experience. Bosses must create boundaries to take advantage of the intellect and corral the immaturity. Through clear directions, a structured approach to the work, and stated expectations, the boss can grow young employees into successful, productive workers.

Don & Gayle

Don, a recent graduate of a technical program, works for an engineer. The engineer, Gayle, has become so accustomed to the work she does that she no longer thinks about it. She has forgotten the many things that she had to learn on the job that were not in her college courses. Now she is the boss and she expects Don to show initiative and get the job done. She believes he has everything he needs to do that—after all, he graduated from a top engineering school. In reality, Don doesn't have a clue. He asks about the tasks and gets condescending looks from Gayle. Frustrated, he just gives the appearance of working. Gayle, recognizing things aren't getting done, begins to think of him as another one of those lazy and uncaring "twenty-somethings."

Keep your frog in your pocket!

If bosses can keep their frogs under control, age—young or old—will not be an issue. The application of sound management principles will be the focus, and the boss will not confuse the educational and maturity levels of employees with their particular performance levels.

Personal Interests

We do what's in our best interest.

"What do people want?" That is one of the most often asked questions by bosses. The answer is simple. They want what they want. They want to get the best deal they can. Some are not able to articulate this as well as others, but the fact is, we are all concerned with satisfying our own interests. That could be money, time off, benefits, training, and so on.

As in any transaction, employees want the maximum return for their efforts. In other words, they want the most for the least! This is natural. They want to get the greatest long term benefits for efforts expended. Does it make any sense to put out more for less? We certainly don't seem to think so when it comes to running our organizations.

It has been estimated that about 50 percent of the work force work just hard enough to keep their jobs. In other words, it is not in their interest to work any harder. An estimated 75 percent of workers think they could be more effective. They, too, are not using their full capacities in the interest of the organization. However, they are operating in their own interests.

Yet we ask, if employees are pursuing their own interests, are they going to be "good" employees? Yes, if their interests are consistent with those of the organization. If the interests of the employees and the organization are not similar, the employees will give priority to their personal interests. We cannot deny that employees do what is in their best interest. It's human nature.

Now you might be thinking, all people want is the easy way. That fits with the results of surveys asking managers what workers want most. Bosses usually respond by saying, "More money and better benefits." But that's not the case. When workers are asked the same questions, they reply: interesting work, a good working environment, fair supervision and opportunities to grow. These are the core things that must be compatible between the organization and the employee. Money comes further down the list for employees. That's why you will see people walk away from good money when the work doesn't match their interests. Or you will find employees who stay in lower-paying jobs because they like the work and the environment.

Businesses spend a great deal of time trying to encourage and motivate employees when, in reality, any motivation has to originate within the employee. Our willingness to give maximum output in a job is predicated on the belief that we will also get the maximum benefit. That means that boss and employee are in agreement as to the value of the work being performed, and there is an alignment between what the boss is seeking and the employee's personal interests.

This issue of alignment is one reason why organizations with a clear vision and purpose are far more successful than those without. It is easier to find employees who fit in the organization when they know up front what the organization stands for.

If we look at the areas where there is the greatest opportunity for conflict between the organization's interests and the employee's, we can identify three broad categories. First, people want equality. They want to feel that they are being treated equally, relative to others. Second, they want security without threats from the organization, bosses and co-workers. And, third, they want to have some control over their life at work.

Anna & Stewart

Anna worked twenty years for a printing company. She did the same job all those years and felt pretty secure. Her boss, Stewart, started talking about getting a computer. Anna's behavior started to become erratic and defensive. Why? On some level, Anna felt that her personal interest, her security, were under threat. How could the boss have introduced the idea without gigging Anna's frog?

Keep your frog in your pocket!

Ask yourself, how do equality, security and control affect your own energy? How do you behave when any one of these three is threatened? Then take a look at your employees.

Do frogs peep over the lily pad in your work place? If so, what changes do you need to make?

Locus of Control

Who's in charge here?

Locus of control is a term used to describe how employees determine what shapes or guides their lives. There are two extremes. First, there are the employees who believe everything comes from within themselves; the events in their lives are the results of choices they make. Then there are the employees who believe that everything comes from outside themselves; the fates control their lives. Few people, if any, are at the two extremes.

Our friend the frog takes its direction from external forces. It can only react. Some people believe they can only react. An example is the person who is dependent on her horoscope. It says, "This is a bad day." So she goes out "knowing" it would be better if she stayed home in bed that day. Everything that happens that day will be perceived as bad. Another example is the person who always blames someone else for his problems or failure. We all know people who believe "if it wasn't for Jane, I could have...."

These are people with a strong external locus of control, or "high externals." They believe what happens to them is a function of luck. They think that all they have to do is wait for "that something" to happen. We know it rarely does. Self-help books appeal to externals, who believe that by reading the books something special will happen. "That something" is usually nothing, because high externals don't act on what they read. They end up waiting on the lily pad.

People with a strong external locus of control look to bosses for direction. They have been socialized to believe they should not take action unless directed by another person. These people will do most of what they are asked to do without question, but do not expect them to initiate action on their own. They do not have this set of habits. It is not that they are incapable, but they prefer to wait for direction.

To people who are externally directed, thinking out of the box has no meaning. There is too much risk, and they have an aversion to risk. Often they are seen as very good workers because they comply. Still, bosses get frustrated with them because they will not go the extra step without being told.

Ben & Alex

Ben has worked for Alex for five years. Until recently, Ben's job was routine. He came to work every day, did his job and let Alex know when he needed help. Recently, new technology was introduced. Ben is constantly having problems and uses much of Alex's time. He seems afraid of making a mistake. In fact, he is. Ben wants Alex to tell him exactly how to do his job and relieve him of any responsibility. When that doesn't happen, Ben's frog gets loose.

If Ben were more internally directed, he would be solving his problems by learning the technology himself and applying his judgment. That, of course, could lead to another set of problems and the eventual stirring of Alex's frog.

Compare Ben to employees with a high internal locus of control. They get their direction from within themselves. People who are high internals believe they control their destiny. It is up to them to take charge of their lives. They do what they think is best. They often question everything and look for new ways to do things.

The high internals look to management to complement their efforts. For example, they want management to assist them in accomplishing their objective by providing resources rather than direction. High internals often test bosses and may be seen as out of control. They may not comply, but they get the work done and need little monitoring. In effect, they manage themselves, and sometimes resent external controls.

The style for directing people with a high external locus of control should be easy. Just determine what you want done and tell them. However, managing those with a high internal locus of control offers you a growth challenge.

Keep your frog in your pocket!

If you are a boss who fears losing control, you may have difficulty letting go enough to keep high internals involved. These employees work best when you let them determine what needs to be done. Then make sure they have what they need to do it.

Part One Summary

We've seen how employee attributes affect performance in the work place. We've also taken a look at how the boss's own attributes may contribute to bringing out the best in the employee or to bringing out the frog.

Attitude. Did you know that if you take the letters of the word attitude, find their numeric position in the alphabet and add them up, you get 100? It takes 100 percent of the right attitudes translated into behaviors that will get the job done.

Creativity. Creativity requires play and a relaxed mind. One famous physicist said all great discoveries originate in the three B's: the bus, the bedroom, or the bath. Decide if you really want creativity in your organization, and if you do, how you can best support it. But be realistic. If you don't really want creativity, don't talk out of both sides of your mouth.

Education vs. Maturity. Bosses can't assume that just because an employee has a Masters Degree in whatever that they are also mature. Immature employees need support, structure, and guidance to be successful.

Personal Interests. The fact that people pursue their personal interests isn't a bad thing. Actually, it's normal and probably healthy, if not carried to the extreme. What is needed is first to hire people with not only good attitudes, but also whose values and personal interests match those of the organization. The closer the fit, the more likely the effort the employee expends will align with the work to be done.

Locus of Control. Are you an internal or an external? What are your employees? Adjust the amount of guidance and direction you give depending on the employee's needs. Not sure? Ask. No, don't ask if they're an internal or external—they'll definitely think the frog is loose. The next time you assign a task, ask, "Do you need me to give you more direction on how to do this, or would you prefer to figure it out yourself?"

Pond-er this

How much time do you spend worrying about an employee's attitude? Describe the behaviors you are observing that make you question this employee's attitude. Are the behaviors affecting the employee's performance? If so, how? Be specific. If you answered yes to these last two questions, how do you plan to address the behaviors?

Do you find yourself talking about being creative or innovative with your staff? Why? How important is creativity to the work that must be done now or in the future? If creativity is important, your first step is to create an environment that supports and nourishes creativity. What will you do?

Do you have any employees that you think are struggling due to their immaturity? If so, describe the immature behaviors you are observing. How could you provide more direction or support? Be specific.

List the goals of your organization and of your department. Then think about your employees and the talents and personal interests of each one. How can you capitalize on these talents and interests? The next time you are interviewing someone, see if you can better discern how their personal interests might fit with the interests of the organization and department.

Who on your staff operates from an external locus of control? Why do you think this? Who operates from an internal locus of control? Again, why do you think so? What changes can you make in your behaviors as a manager that may be helpful to either kind of employee?

In the Performance Formula, it is not just the employee's attributes that affect the work that gets done. In the next section we examine energy and its impact on performance.

In the Performance Formula, it is not just the employee's attributes that affect the work that gets done.

Energy is required to propel the work. The form of the energy can be centered on the boss or on the individual worker.

Part Two

Performance =
Employee Attributes x
Energy x
the Boss

In Part Two, we examine Energy:

Structure
Motivation

Why can't these employees work as hard as me?

Structure

We seek structure in order to avoid uncertainty.

People seem to have a natural need for order and structure. The degree of need may vary, but people need to know where they stand and the boundaries within which they operate.

What is structure? In management, structure relates to how much things need to be spelled out. Is a job description required that clearly details job duties and responsibilities? Does the boss have to check work frequently to make sure the employee is headed in the right direction and on time? Does the employee need someone else to lay out the steps in order to accomplish a task? The more these things are provided, the more structure there is. Even a strategic plan is a part of the structure.

All employees need structure. The problem is, many bosses go to one extreme or the other—all structure or none—without considering how much their employees actually need. Too much structure can throttle energy that feeds motivation, initiative, and creativity. Too little can result in time wasted, duplicated effort, and confusion about the job—in other words, wasted energy.

How much structure an employee needs is related to their knowledge and experience with a task. A 15-year veteran employee may still not know how to use a new piece of equipment and may need the "structure" of a training class, as well as observation during the learning period. Give that same employee a piece of equipment or a task she is familiar with and stand back. More than likely she just needs you to get out of the way.

New employees need structure. Too many of them suffer from the "sink or swim" approach to orientation and a new position. Bosses throw them in and then complain that they aren't performing up to standards. Even if new employees have done the job before, they haven't done it in your organization. They need you to provide the structure as they learn the ropes.

In addition, different people have different needs for structure. Some people like to define their own structure. In other words, given a goal or a result to achieve, they have the skills, knowledge, experience and desire to go off and make it happen. Others with the same attributes are more reluctant to take off. They sometimes need a nudge. Recall the earlier discussion about locus of control.

Karen & Matt

Karen's boss was out of town. Frustrated because her boss, Matt, didn't tell her what to do while he was out, Karen did nothing. In essence, she waited for something to happen. She hopped without accomplishing anything. When she came home that evening her husband asked her what she had done all day. She replied, "Nothing." The next day Matt asked Karen why she had not done a set of reports. She responded, "You didn't tell me to do those reports. How was I to know what you wanted done?" What do you think happened to Matt's frog?

Keep your frog in your pocket!

You may think this sounds like a guessing game, but really all it takes is some honest discussion. Sit down with the employee and ask some questions to determine the level of knowledge about an assignment. Together assess the employee's knowledge, his gaps and what he will need. No need to guess—just ask. What happens when structure is needed and it is not provided? The frog starts to randomly move. People tend to want to do something, so hopping is the natural reaction. Take action to avoid unwelcome circumstances.

Motivation

Is it motivation or obedience?

Some of you may be excited to come to this section. Maybe you'll finally get the answer you've been waiting for. How do I get these employees eager to do their work?

Stop right there. Before you go any further, you need to determine whether you are really concerned about motivation or obedience. In most cases, your complaint is not about motivation, but an employee failing to do what you told them to—that's about obedience. Obedience requires a different frame of reference than motivation. Obedience is usually what brings out frog-like, reactionary behaviors.

If you want motivation, are you prepared to give employees the free rein they need and allow them to pursue clearly agreed upon goals as they see fit? Better answer this question before yelling, "These employees aren't motivated!" It's up to you to be sure that the goals are clear and the employee understands them.

Are your expectations clear? Does the employee have the skills and knowledge needed to perform successfully? Often we operate on assumptions in the area of skills. We assume that an employee knows how to do the job.

Once your expectations are clear, the employee has agreed to take on the job, and you know the employee has the skills needed, then if the work isn't getting done, you have an obedience problem. Dealing with the failure of an employee to obey or get the job done requires discipline and consistency on the boss's part—a hard task for many of us. It takes guts to stick to your guns and follow the organization's policies until you've either convinced the employee that he needs to change or to move to an environment better suited to his mode of operation, that is, to some other organization.

But how do you know when you're dealing with a motivation problem? If we look at one of the earliest theories of motivation, we can begin to assess the answer to this question. Abraham Maslow developed a pyramid of needs which must be met progressively in order for a person to perform.

Maslow's pyramid starts with basic needs a person must have in order to survive, such as food and shelter. The pyramid then proceeds through security needs, self-esteem needs, socialization needs and finally self-actualization needs (being "all that you can be," like the U.S. Army recruitment jingle).

Obviously, if you're near the bottom of the pyramid worrying about security, it's more difficult to stay excited about a job. Most bosses tend to think that would make a person want to do really superb work, but it tends to have the opposite effect. The employee is simply too distracted and worried. When the basic needs of survival are met, a person begins to have a greater sense of motivation toward the types of achievement we usually think of in the work place.

Jason & Marcus

Jason had been a model employee. He did everything he was asked to do in the way he was told to do it. But technology changed his job. Perhaps the changes came overnight, and like the frog in the boiling water, he hopped out, thinking things would change. Now he can't seem to get anything done and has all kinds of excuses. Jason has been hopping around aimlessly. Marcus, his boss, doesn't know what to do with him.

Is motivation the problem? Maybe he had been used to being obedient. Clearly something is wrong. Has he been trained to do his job? Is he being told what to do? Jason needs structure. He needs support. He may come around to functioning without Marcus's help, but why not help him out?

Keep your frog in your pocket!

Tell him what he must do and how to do it and then monitor his performance. When he does well, let him know. Otherwise, he will meander and the next thing you know, your own frog will start hopping.

To keep things simple, when you're concerned about motivation or the lack of it, approach the issues with these questions in mind:

- How is structure (or lack of it) affecting performance?
- Is the employee secure?
- Is the employee being paid equitably?
- Was the employee previously able to do the work?
- Would training help?

Part Two Summary

In this section, we have taken a look at energy. Most likely there are many other factors involved, but the two we chose are critical.

Structure. Providing the what and the how of doing a job is providing structure. Even the most experienced employee needs structure, the what and the how, when it's time to do a new task.

Motivation. In *The One Minute Manager*, Ken Blanchard describes motivation as a combination of confidence and commitment. Confidence is the belief that you can do the job; commitment is the willingness or desire to do it. To increase confidence, we must increase the support and encouragement we provide the employee. To increase commitment, we must increase the structure and direction we give.

Some more things to pond-er

Think of a recent assignment you gave to one of your employees. How much structure did you provide? Did you provide adequate detail about what was needed and why it was needed? Was this task new for the employee, or something he or she had done before? What were the results? If you got less than optimum results, perhaps more structure was needed. Perhaps the employee needed more direction, not only about the what and why, but also about the how.

Do you think your employees are motivated to do the work? Why, or why not? Be specific. Where motivation doesn't seem as high as you would like, think about whether you are looking at an employee who lacks confidence or one who lacks commitment. If there is a lack of confidence, are there ways to bolster the confidence? Do you need to provide more direction and structure in order to increase commitment? What actions can you take?

In the next section, we will look at the boss and how he or she affects performance.

In the Performance Formula, the boss brings the capacity to capture the energy and employee attributes.

The tools and mindset are determined by the boss.

Part Three

Performance =
Employee Attributes x
Energy x
the Boss

In Part Three, we examine the Boss:

Experience
Teams
Diversity
Self-Fulfilling Prophecy
Communication
Trust

YOU make the difference.

Experience

Know thyself

There's nothing like experience to put things and people in a different perspective. A boss at one year has a totally different way of seeing and reacting than a boss after ten years, or even five years.

It's like children. At age 10 or 11 they think they know more than their parents do. New bosses often think they have all of the answers and know the right way to get things done. It takes experience and seasoning for them to realize there's more than one way, and there actually might be some better ways.

As you read in Part One, we often confuse education and maturity. Many businesses today admit the mistake of hiring people directly out of business school for key leadership roles. They recognize that business schools don't usually address human relations, the key component of leadership. The schools focus on accounting and finance and economics, critical elements of running a business. Yet, as any experienced boss knows, there is a lot more to running a successful business than being able to run the numbers.

It seems that experience and maturity are the best process for leaders, enabling them to increase their skills for understanding the "people element" of work. It's not so much a function of age as it is the opportunity to practice in the field of human relations.

With seasoning, good managers develop greater tolerance of the wide variability in human nature. Hopefully, we learn to appreciate differences and recognize the value those differences bring to our work team. This is true of managers at any age. Managers benefit from working their way up through the organization, gaining experience in those areas where they can do the least damage as they grow and learn.

Kevin & the Coach

Kevin is a new manager, and he is frustrated. He just can't seem to get himself together. He doesn't like his job, his boss or his employees. When asked why by his newly acquired coach, he can't come up with a clear explanation. He doesn't know that he behaves like a frog, reacting to folks in ways that get frog-like responses.

His coach suggests that until Kevin can crystallize the core of his problems, his difficulties will continue. She also suggests that he start with himself and recognize how he contributes to the problems. Then she adds that one of the best things he can do is develop a thorough knowledge and understanding of himself.

The coach suggests that Kevin keep a log of his performance similar to the ones he might keep on his employees. In the log he describes any significant events that occur during the day along with how he feels about them. The log serves as a concrete way to examine his contributions to desirable, as well as unwanted, results.

Keep your frog in your pocket!

Try this yourself. Take a few minutes at the end of each day to describe what went well and what didn't go so well. Include any significant interactions with others.

Be sure to write how you felt or are feeling. Do this for one month. Then go back and review your documentation. See any patterns? See any changes you want to make? Are there days when your behavior resembles a frog's? Work on these things and keep writing.

Teams

The Seven Dwarves

Working in teams is a big issue today. Teamwork is now considered to be the standard for working relationships. But putting a bunch of people together and calling them a team isn't automatically going to work. Most bosses don't have experience managing this way.

The boss reads an article about the success of teams and decides—BAM—that's how the work place will operate from now on. He brings in a consultant, spends a few days on training and turns the teams loose. It might not be quite this poorly planned, but it can feel that way, and the results can be dismal.

Too often we fail to understand team development. Without direction, groups fall into such traps as: (1) unclear or confusing goals; (2) different, often conflicting, individual interests; (3) unclear task obligations; or (4) lack of management direction. Any or all of these traps lead to dysfunctional outcomes such as low productivity, in-fighting, anger or confusion. In addition, employees often just don't trust management's commitment to teams.

When properly constituted, teams offer the advantages of greater cooperation, output and problem-solving capacity. They also are able to self-manage. To gain these advantages, it is critical to carefully select team members. As you review who is needed for the team, think about the goal to be accomplished, membership relations, communication patterns, the level of management support, and the reward system.

Even if you select the greatest people ever for the team, team training will be essential to bridging the gap between individual effort and team effort. If we think of training as practice, the benefits are more obvious. The cost of practice is usually far less than the cost of failure.

Evan, Jen, Josh, & the Team

Teams were formed. Rah, Rah, Rah. Members gathered together in their teams and looked at one another. The common question was, "We're a team now—what do we do differently?" That question unanswered, the members went on doing what they had been doing and responding when the team name was called. Evan never talked to team members. Jen blamed all problems on "this new team stuff." Josh had never played a team sport and had no idea what anyone was talking about. The result was a frog farm.

Keep your frog in your pocket!

Think before you leap! Teams aren't always the right choice. They take time and cause role confusion. Most of all they require people to change. If you're not personally ready to make the changes required to work as part of a team, then don't impose it on your employees. Be wary of creating a frog farm.

Diversity

We choose people we're comfortable with.

Because we choose people we're already familiar with, we rarely get comfortable with people who are different. The more we expose ourselves to different people, the more we are able to see how we are alike versus how we are different. How diverse is your organization? Studies show that heterogeneous groups bring broader solutions to problems. And what organization today couldn't use broader solutions?

What is diversity? It is including people of both genders and different races, religions, and cultures in the organization. The key word here is "including." Though most companies today have at least some employees who are "different," the problem seems to lie in minorities being left out of problem-solving and decision-making roles.

It is a rare organization that serves only one element of our population. So if you were providing a service or a product to a diverse population, wouldn't you want to have access to more knowledge about that population? Who knows better than the employees who belong to that group?

Use the word diversity and watch mouths drop open and faces wrinkle. Let's look at a cultural difference. In one subculture, eye contact between peers is considered appropriate. The listener maintains contact toward the sender who is allowed eye variability. In another subculture, the listener is not supposed to look at the sender. Mix cultures and what happens?

Both senders will, no doubt, make assumptions about the

listeners. Neither might be correct. Who says listening has anything to do with eye contact, other than habit? Before you jump onto your lily pad in disagreement, answer this question: What eye contact exists in a telephone conversation?

Our lack of understanding of diversity issues only causes the frog population to multiply. As that happens, the job of the boss becomes more complicated as many of the issues are emotional, yet camouflaged by other problems, rather than the real one—this person is different from me and I don't understand him and that makes me uncomfortable.

Diversity challenge

Getting diverse groups to work together successfully can be a bit of a challenge, but as with many things that are accepted in an organization, it all starts at the top and moves down through management. What do your actions say? How does your top management group look? One person described it as "beige." Do you have policies in place that reinforce valuing differences?

You may be wondering about the value of diversity training. Such training seems to get mixed results. If you decide to offer it, choose carefully. Make sure you select a trainer or a consultant whose goal is to create cooperation and not dissent. Be wary of one-day training programs. One day will not change a lifetime of behaviors. It will take follow-up training and, of course, support from management.

Keep your frog in your pocket!

One place to start making changes is in yourself. Challenge your comfort zone by volunteering to work in a setting outside the norm for yourself. Serve on a board for an ethnic or opposite gender organization, tutor children from a disadvantaged neighborhood, or serve meals at a shelter for the homeless. As you stretch your exposure to persons from different backgrounds, you will find your own perceptions and acceptance shifting and your frog staying in your pocket.

Self-Fulfilling Prophecy

A rose is a rose.

Remember the play My Fair Lady? Liza Doolittle was transformed from a lowly flower girl into a lady when Higgins believed in her. His belief, along with some training and coaching, made all the difference.

There have been numerous studies of the self-fulfilling prophecy. One study in education involved telling a teacher that a group of students were gifted. In reality, these were kids who normally didn't do very well. As the school year went by, the students exceeded their previous performance levels. The only difference was a teacher who believed she was working with gifted students. How can this happen?

We all live up to expectations, whether they are our own internal expectations or someone else's. We work as hard as we need to meet a standard of success—no more, no less. So what does all of this have to do with management?

Unrealistic expectations

Do your employees know what you expect from them? Do you believe they will be successful, or have you thrown your hands in the air and given up? Do they clearly know the goals, the standards they must meet, in order to be productive? Try this test: go to each of your employees and say to him or her, "Tell me what the standards are for your work. What do you need to do in order to be rated outstanding in…." You pick the categories. If they can answer clearly without hesitation, you've done your job. If they can't, then get busy.

Now what happens when an employee understands the expectations, but isn't doing the job? First of all, ask yourself if the employee has the skills needed. Has he been able to perform the job in the past? If the answer is yes, then you need to address whatever underlying issues are preventing the expected performance. Restate your expectations and get the employee's input on improvements. If the answer is no, then provide the training and structure he needs to acquire the skills while clarifying expectations.

Keep your frog in your pocket!

Whatever you do, don't let the employee be a frog, hopping around aimlessly, if you know the way he should be heading.

Communication

Hello. Anybody there?

How many times have you complained about an employee who just didn't get it? It seems like no matter how many times you explain an assignment or task, you don't get the results you're looking for. You complain about the employee's lack of initiative or slowness or whatever. Unfortunately, too often we are quick to blame the employee rather than ourselves and our lack of clear communication.

Always remember that communication is a process. It involves the sending and receiving of a message. The outcome serves as feedback. If the outcome is what you expected, then you've been successful in communicating. If you don't like the outcome, focus on what may have gone wrong in the communication process as the issue, rather than on the employee—at least to start with.

Remember, you initiate the communication because you want something to happen. You get feedback that it doesn't. The feedback is telling you the input has to be changed. You are the input mechanism. So, if you want to correct the situation, don't wait for someone to read your mind. You need to make your wishes clear.

More often than not, we assume that others understand us exactly as we intend. Usually there is a big gap between intent and understanding. Simple words, for example, have multiple meanings. What does "soon" mean? Or "later?" Or "quickly?" The meanings are different for each of us. "Get me this as soon as possible" leaves lots of room for interpretation—and disappointment.

Next time you give an employee an assignment, take a few minutes at the end and check his understanding. Ask him to restate your request so you can immediately correct misunderstandings. The result will be twofold. You increase the probability of getting what you want and avoid a lot of negative emotion later.

You can never over-communicate. Often, bosses make an announcement at a staff meeting and assume everyone heard what was said. The problem is, people's minds will wander. If they happen to wander at the wrong moment, they may lose an important announcement, unless the boss has enough sense to repeat it.

Write that important announcement on a flip chart and stand it beside you during the meeting. Have someone at the end of the meeting summarize the important points. (Of course, you want to let people know you are going to do this before you start the meeting.) Follow up with a memo. Post it on the bulletin board. Put in it in a newsletter. The more critical the information, the more often employees need to hear it and see it.

Math class

Remember math class? The teacher would go over a concept. We didn't understand and would ask for the explanation again. She obliged by giving it in the same words and in the same way. The result? We still didn't understand. Soon she would become exasperated. Frog time! She told us we needed to pay attention and to listen. Paying attention was not the issue. We just didn't understand what she was saying. If she had tried another way and a new set of words or frame of reference, we might have had a chance.

Keep your frog in your pocket!

Communication is a pond of opportunity for frogs. The frogs come out because we do not understand the process and its components. Nor do we take the time to improve. We know exactly what we have said and expect others to understand. Yet, they don't more often than they do. It's a wonder we don't see more aimless hopping.

Trust

I don't know, there's just something about him I don't trust.

For most people, trust means: "I can depend on your word and your actions and that you will do what you say."

Trust as a sense or feeling becomes the foundation for cooperation and mutual respect. In turn, it allows us to move in the same direction as another with confidence. Critical to a trusting relationship is honesty.

Trust and honesty are so tightly linked that one does not exist without the other. We always have a choice of whether we are honest or dishonest in our communication with others. It is easy to be seduced into dishonesty and even self-deception. It allows us to avoid conflict, to protect ourselves, or to gain an advantage. Dishonesty is a risky act that has little consequence until it is uncovered. Then look out. Trust is destroyed.

Often organizations encourage lies. It starts with little things, like building extra into the budget, to things like telling customers you'll have a product ready on a date that you know isn't going to happen.

What happens in these cases when you tell the truth? You create what you believe is a realistic budget. However, you soon face a boss who tells you it's too much and you need to cut it. No further explanation is provided. You tell your boss, "I can't cut this budget! These numbers are realistic." The boss says, "Cut it anyway." What happened here? A breakdown in trust? In communication? In expectations? Next year, you're prepared. You pad the budget, expecting the cuts. Thus a cycle of dishonesty and distrust has been born.

What about the customer situation? If you tell the customer the truth about a delay in a delivery and he takes his business somewhere else, your boss sends you on your way. It's as if honesty doesn't pay. Talk about stress!

If you are considered a trustworthy person, dishonesty is out of the question, even when the consequences are unpleasant. Trusted people are seen as a source of inspiration and help. With the resulting respect and dignity, they take followers in the right direction. The culture of the organization becomes invested in doing the right thing, or "walking the talk."

Erosion of trust

Trust can easily be destroyed by one simple thought, the idea that you cannot trust another person. That thought may come from an action, a glimpse or a rumor. We cannot control the thoughts of others, but we can behave in ways that minimize the impact of such thoughts. In addition, we have to be wary of negative self-fulfilling prophecies. We must not allow the negative thoughts of others to justify behaviors inconsistent with building trust. Where trust does not exist, frogs proliferate. You know the behaviors. Get even and get even fast. Get the best lily pad and keep it.

Keep your frog in your pocket!

If we look at sustaining performance, trust between bosses and employees serves as the foundation. Trust enables leaders to influence their followers.

Just remember, **TRUST** is:

- Truthful and open communication
- Respect for others' opinions, capabilities, differences
- Unlimited patience
- Searching to resolve differences
- Teaching others so they can do their best

To talk about trust is easy. Actions are what count!

Part Three Summary

There is so much that the boss can do that will ultimately influence employee performance.

Experience. It takes a seasoned individual to understand human behavior. "Seasoned" doesn't necessarily mean older, but it does mean experienced. Experience helps develop empathy for the situations in which employees find themselves. Through experience, the boss knows how to get Ed to come around in his work, or how important it is to listen to Susan for just a few extra minutes. He knows he'll get that much more work from her with just a small investment of time.

Teams. All the cheering in the world won't create a successful team. Bosses often confuse teams and teamwork. You can have teamwork without actually being a team. Teamwork is about cooperation and helping each other out. Don't jump at putting a team together unless the situation calls for it and be sure to pick the right people—especially the right leader.

Diversity. Different folks, different ideas. Diversity is one of the most talked about business topics today. Few organizations are willing to take all the steps necessary to ensure the inclusion of diverse groups in their efforts. However, every boss can take the first steps to ensure their own openness to diverse people.

Self-Fulfilling Prophecy. What you see is what you get, at least in one sense. If you see potential for greatness in your employees and treat them accordingly, that's what you'll get.

Communication. Ribbet! Frog talk. Communication is one of the most complicated processes we must use as bosses. Yet, it is also the one that people pay the least attention to improving. If every boss would work on this one skill, the increase in productivity would be phenomenal.

Trust. Such a little word carries so much power. Never underestimate how much employees watch to see if what you do matches what you say. Watching you is how they learn to stay safe in the environment, how they learn what it takes to succeed.

Even more things to pond-er

How have your interactions with employees changed over the years as you have gained experience? If they have not changed much, seek out feedback to help you see where you might need to make changes. Ask a trusted colleague for feedback. Ask someone from human resources to interview your staff. Or ask your staff directly, if you have built a relationship that allows them to feel comfortable giving you feedback.

Have you been talking about being a team? Decide now if you are really after a team, or if you would just like for people to cooperate and treat each other with respect. If you really want to pursue a team structure, do some research, be willing to give up some of your authority, and prepare to provide some training.

Who among your staff do you not expect much from? How has this come to be? How might you be reinforcing his or her poor performance? What could you do differently?

What have you done to increase your comfort with people

of different backgrounds? What will you do?

How good do you think you are at communicating? Would your staff agree? Would they say you listen carefully to what they have to say, or do you grudgingly lend an ear while tending to other things? Increase your awareness of what you are doing when someone is talking to you. Ask for feedback from your family or friends about your listening skills. They will give you a good idea of what your staff might say.

Does your staff trust you? How do you know? Would you trust you? Be specific in your answers.

Performance Formula Recap

Whew! Here we are. The formula is completed and the results are in. Now you know why

Employee Attributes x Energy x the Boss = Performance

We started out with the attributes that employees bring to the organization, but as you see, they can't do it alone. Remember, it isn't you, and it isn't me. It's us. While the Performance Formula is simple, with only three variables, we know it takes desire, practice and commitment to get the maximum out of it. When any one variable is low, performance drops.

It is sad to hear managers say, "If you can't do it, I'll find someone who can," or, "If you aren't happy here, then go somewhere else." If you hear those words, you know the frogs have taken over. We, the authors of this book, are not trying to be Pollyannas, suggesting there is never a problem employee in the work place. All of us behave like frogs at times, and some people don't know any other way to behave. We only caution you not to let your frog dictate your own behavior.

What we are asking is that you believe that you can increase your success by reducing frog-like behaviors, both your own and those of your employees. Your ability—or inability—to keep your frog in your pocket seriously impacts the ability of your employees to do the same. When you or one of your employees is being a frog, back up and look at what is happening. Ask yourself where in the Performance Formula things have gone wrong. Then choose to change that variable or compensate with another one. You don't have to be reactive, and you don't have to be a frog.

Keep your frog in your pocket!

Now you understand the dangers of the frog. Capture your frog, solve problems, and deal with people using the Performance Formula, and you will make the "leap" from boss to leader.

30 Frog-like Behaviors

Reactive froglike behaviors

Needs to be told what to do
Waits for something to happen
Is easily distracted
Is easily stressed
Resists changes

Escalates conflict
Focuses on getting even
Rejects new information
Holds onto grudges
Second-guesses others

Non-Adaptive froglike behaviors

Pines for the old days
Is stuck in a rut
Has a "poor me" attitude
Wants things done in a particular fussy way
Has "not invented here" attitude

Avoids risk
Seldom asks for assistance
Prefers old ways
Likes information consistent with beliefs
Knows what's wrong with others

Undirected froglike behaviors

Seldom initiates efforts
Avoids work
Has "not my job" response
Is oblivious to others
Fears failure

Fails to develop new skill sets
Is predictable
Can't see ahead
Remembers the bad

Other Works by Dr. Wally

Learn more about Dr. Wally Johnston and where to buy his books, videos, audio recordings by visiting www.askdrwally.com.

In Paperback
  Speaking of Work
  What Every Boss Needs to Know: Learning to Keep your Frog
    in your Pocket

On DVD
  Working Smart
  The Metaphor of the Frog

On CD/audiocassette
  Messages for Self

Frog tokens

Cut out these tokens and keep them in your pocket to remind yourself: **Keep your frog in your pocket!** ✂

www.ingramcontent.com/pod-product-compliance
Lightning Source LLC
Chambersburg PA
CBHW031536210526
45464CB00003B/1039